D0124212

# Punctuation Celebration

by
ELSA KNIGHT BRUNO

illustrated by
JENNY WHITEHEAD

SQUARE FISH
HENRY HOLT AND COMPANY
NEW YORK

What, race?
Punctuation Field Day
— 50-Yard Dash —
Parenthesis Jump Rope
3-Legged Race
Finish
Go, Dash!

# Field Day Frolic

On your marks!

Get set!

Let's go!

To a sporty exploration

Into words and punctuation.

We'll meet the players, learn each name,

And celebrate this special game.

The period is just a dot
Found sitting in its favorite spot.
When a sentence ends, it comes and plops,
And where it plops, the sentence STOPS.

It also can abbreviate
An address, first name, size, or weight
(Like lb. for pound, ft. for feet,
Doz. for dozen, and St. for street).

*Elizabeth and little Jay*
*Bought two doz. eggs today,*
*One lb. of cheese,*
*And nonstick spray*
*At the Delany St. Café.*

What is a question mark?

When do you need it?

Where do you put it?

How do you read it?

A question mark is apropos

When there are things you want to know.

You put it after words that ask.

To answer is another's task.

A present for me?
Can I give it a squeeze?
Can I pull off the ribbons?
Can I open it, please?
BUD

The exclamation point has clout.

HIP! HIP! HOORAY!

STRIKE THREE! YOU'RE OUT!

It fires you up, there is no doubt.

The symbol means you have to SHOUT!

*Annie crawled under*
*When she heard the thunder,*
*Along with some dust and a spider.*
*KA-BOOM!*
*There's nothing more frightening*
*Than listening to lightning,*
*Unless it's that spider beside her.*
*EEEK! EEEK!*

# Comma

The comma is common
And commonly used
To separate clauses
With essential pauses.

Don't want to confuse you,
But think you should know,
It does not say "Stop."
It simply says "Slow."

Please use it whenever
You're writing the date,
Words in a series,
And cities with states.

Today, March 1,
I boarded a train
In sleet, snow, and rain
For Bar Harbor, Maine.
BAR HARBOR
MAINE

# Apostrophe

Alas, the poor apostrophe
Has two big jobs, it seems to me.
In order to help words possess,
It tags along and adds an "s"
(Like Mickey's mess or Della's dress).

And when one word, not two, is better,
It happily replaces letters.
Whatever's left is not a fraction.
We'll call the new word a contraction
(Like can't or we'll or it's or she'll).

*Mickey made a mighty mess,*
*Spilling paint on Della's dress.*
*Now it's being washed and pressed.*

Quotation marks come two by two.
Use two before, two when you're through.
Enclosed are words said by another,
Like, *"Clean this messy room!"* yelled Mother.
Or
*"Fourscore and seven years ago . . ."*
Who said those words?
I'll bet you know!

"Four-
score
and
seven
years
ago..."
Abraham
Lincoln
"You
were
right!"

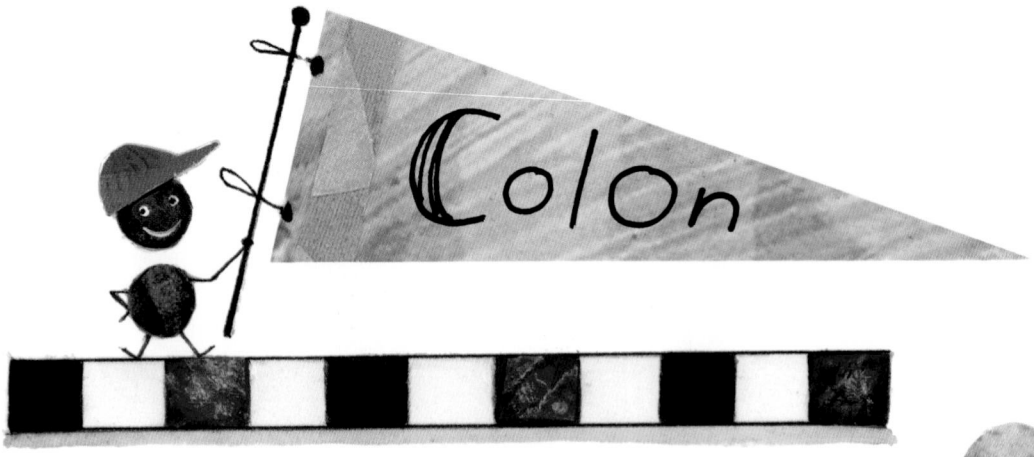


The colon is quite stubborn,
And always will insist
It be the one and only one
To introduce a list.

Another use, when telling time,
No matter how you spin it,
At 6:30 it separates
The hours from the minutes.

*I shook my blue jeans upside down.*
*Both pockets emptied, these I found:*
*Some cookie crumbs, a plastic spoon,*
*A box of raisins from last June,*
*Two gum balls, and a red balloon.*
*We'd better wash my blue jeans soon!*

Semicolon
The semicolon separates
Two sentences, if they relate.
Party
11:30
Invite
HAPPY

Tomorrow's my birthday; I'm going to be seven.

I'm having a party at half past eleven.

Ten friends are invited; I am so excited!

Parentheses' two hands are gentle,
Enclosing words that aren't essential.

*At lunch, my friends asked me to trade*
*My chocolate milk for lemonade,*
*My super sub (from Barney's deli)*
*For pita bread with gloppy jelly.*
*My deviled eggs (Mom makes the best)*
*For sour grapes (that I detest).*
*Mom always told us we should share.*
*Tomorrow I'm not sitting there!*

Ellipsis points . . . three tiny dots . . .

Are perfect for those silent spots.

Their use, dear reader, is permitted

When certain phrases are omitted.

*Well . . . I wonder . . . could it be*

*That rainbows come out just for me?*

# Dash

The dash—a punctuation mark—
Is more casual than a comma.
So I prefer to think it is
A comma in pajamas!

Oops! I had better mention this.
Remember when you read it,
A dash is used to emphasize
The words that will precede it.

*One thing I must tell you—*
*Not one, there are two—*
*I'm glad I am me,*
*And I'm glad you are you!*

Don't let hyphen fool you.
A dash, it is not.
This poem will remind you,
In case you forgot.

To form compound words
It sometimes is found
Like tom-tom and T-shirt,
And merry-go-round.

Also you should know, some-
times it will appear
And split up a word when
A line end is near.

Who is stronger?
Who will win?
Let the fun and games begin!

But period was soon to fall.
It happened when it kicked the ball.

First it tripped and then it plopped
And that is when the playing stopped.

Words took note and congregated.
Soon a sentence was created.

One by one, each punctuation
Ran to its preferred location.

Sentences were dancing, laughing,
Joining hands, and paragraphing.

Let's WIN!
team
let's
play
the
game
Con-
gre-
gate!
Woo
Woo!

Words went whirling by, enraptured.
Paragraphs were being chaptered.

And, with not a word to spare,
Stories piled up everywhere!

Happy fans rushed from the stands.
All were cheering, clapping hands.

When the dust cleared it revealed
Readers on the playing field!

Mixing words and punctuation—
It's a winning combination!

SQUARE FISH
An imprint of Macmillan Publishing Group, LLC

PUNCTUATION CELEBRATION. Text copyright © 2009 by Elsa Knight Bruno.
Illustrations copyright © 2009 by Jenny Whitehead.
All rights reserved. Printed in China by RR Donnelley Asia Printing Solutions Ltd., Dongguan City, Guangdong Province. For information, address Square Fish, 175 Fifth Avenue, New York, NY 10010.

Square Fish and the Square Fish logo are trademarks of Macmillan and are used by Henry Holt and Company under license from Macmillan.

Library of Congress Cataloging-in-Publication Data
Bruno, Elsa Knight.
Punctuation celebration / Elsa Knight Bruno ; illustrated by Jenny Whitehead.
ISBN 978-1-250-00335-5
1. English language—Punctuation—Juvenile literature. I. Whitehead, Jenny. II. Title.
PE1450.B726 2009 428.2—dc22 2008018337

Originally published in the United States by Christy Ottaviano Books/Henry Holt and Company.
First Square Fish Edition: July 2012. Square Fish logo designed by Filomena Tuosto.
The artist used gouache and cut paper on 90-lb. Arches watercolor paper to create the illustrations for this book.
mackids.com

3 5 7 9 10 8 6 4 2

AR: 3.4 / LEXILE: 650L

Punctuation marks come alive in this clever picture book featuring fourteen playful poems. Periods stop sentences in a baker's shop, commas help a train slow down, quotation marks tell people what to do, and colons stubbornly introduce lists. So come take part in the punctuation celebration!
IRA Teachers' Choice Award
"Here's a poetic way to learn punctuation. . . . Playfully instructive."
—USA Today
SQUARE FI
AN IMPRINT OF MACM
175 FIFTH AVENUE, NEW YORK, N
MACKI
PRINTED I
AGES 6–9
US $7.99 / CAN $11.50
ISBN 978-1-250-00335-5
50799 >
9 781250 003355
P9-BXZ-716